Created, published, and distributed by Knock Knock
1635-B Electric Ave.
Venice, CA 90291
knockknockstuff.com
Knock Knock is a registered trademark of Knock Knock LLC

This book is a work of parody meant solely for entertainment purposes. The quotes in this book are not to be construed as real.

In no event will Knock Knock be liable to any reader for any harm, injury, or damages, including direct, indirect, incidental, special, consequential, or punitive arising out of or in connection with the use of the information contained in this book. So there.

Where specific company, product, and brand names are cited, copyright and trademarks associated with these names are property of their respective owners. Every reasonable attempt has been made to identify owners of copyright. Errors or omissions will be corrected in subsequent editions.

ISBN: 978-160106830-9
UPC: 825703-50159-9

10 9 8 7 6 5 4 3 2 1

This Is
Like, Totally
a Quote Book

KNOCK
KNOCK®
VENICE, CALIFORNIA

This book is dedicated to the eminent individuals whose words are parodied herein. We'd like to imagine each of them, living or dead, getting a chuckle out of it. We only wish we could invite them all to dinner.* That would be, like, totally an amazing party.

*Except maybe Hannibal Lecter.

God said, Let there be light: and there was, like, totally light.

—Genesis 1:3

You may say
I'm a dreamer, but
I'm, like, totally
not the only one.

—John Lennon

I am like totally your father.

—Darth Vader, *The Empire Strikes Back*

BIG BROTHER IS WATCHING YOU.

—George Orwell

TOTALLY, LIKE,

I'm totally not OK and you're totally not OK, and that's, like, totally OK.

—William Sloane Coffin

I, like, totally
did not have
sexual relations
with that woman.

—Bill Clinton

Like, totally call me Ishmael.

—Herman Melville

I like totally pity the fool.

—Mr. T

A house divided against itself totally cannot, like, stand.

—Abraham Lincoln

'Tis totally better to have
loved and lost than, like,
never to have loved at all.

—Alfred Lord Tennyson

I've fallen and I like totally can't get up.

—LifeCall

You only live once, but if you do it right, once is, like, totally enough.

—Mae West

Billie Jean is, like, totally not my lover.

—Michael Jackson

We totally choose to go to the moon in this decade and do the other things, not because they are easy, but because they are like, totally hard.

—John F. Kennedy

You totally can
if you totally think
you totally can.

—Norman Vincent Peale

Sing us a song, you're, like, totally the piano man.

—Billy Joel

The course of true
love never did run,
like, totally smooth.

—William Shakespeare

Thou shalt totally
not commit adultery.

—Exodus 20:14

It's amazing when you li
and you think it's great,
the actors say the words
like, **totally** terrible.

—Spike Lee

write something
t when you hear
lot of times it's,

We'll always, like, totally have Paris.

—Rick Blaine, *Casablanca*

I went over the complete inventory of US nuclear warheads, which is really, like, a totally sobering experience.

—Jimmy Carter

If your dreams do not, like, totally scare you, they are totally not big enough.

—Ellen Johnson Sirleaf

People rarely succeed
at anything unless
they like totally
have fun doing it.

—Dale Carnegie

When I get that feeling I totally want, like, sexual healing.

—Marvin Gaye

That's one totally small step for a man, one, like, totally giant leap for mankind.

—Neil Armstrong

We love to
fly and it like
totally shows.

—Delta Airlines

The best part of married life is totally the fights. The rest is merely, like, so-so.

—Thornton Wilder

All the things I really like to do are either immoral, illegal, or, like, totally fattening.

—Alexander Woollcott

I did not just fall in love. I totally made, like, a parachute jump.

—Zora Neale Hurston

Give me your tired,
your poor, your
huddled masses,
like, totally yearning
to breathe free.

—Emma Lazarus

After all, tomorrow is, like, totally another day.

—Scarlett O'Hara, *Gone with the Wind*

I hate vegetarians, and I, like, totally hate health food.

—Julia Child

Virginia
is totally
for lovers.

—The Virginia State Travel Service

I totally ate his
with some fava
and, like, a nic

—Hannibal Lecter, *The Silence of the Lambs*

iver
beans
Chianti.

Housekeeping, like, totally ain't no joke.

—Louisa May Alcott

Tramps like us, baby, we were, like, totally born to run.

—Bruce Springsteen

You like totally have to know what sparks the light in you so that you, in your own way, can like totally illuminate the world.

—Oprah Winfrey

Louie Louie,
me totally
gotta, like, go.

—The Kingsmen

Hate cannot drive out hate:
like, only love can do that. Totally.

—Dr. Martin Luther King, Jr.

Speak softly
and carry, like,
a totally big stick.

—Theodore Roosevelt

Whatever does not kill me, like, totally makes me stronger.

—Friedrich Nietzsche

I'll, like, totally
be back.

—"The Terminator," *The Terminator*

I am totally strong.
I am totally invincible.
I am totally woman.

—Helen Reddy

To me, old age is always totally, like, fifteen years older than I am.

—Bernard Baruch

The responsibility of great states is to like serve and not to, like, totally dominate the world.

—Harry S. Truman

Like, my greatest strength is that I totally have no weaknesses.

—John McEnroe

Somewhere over
the rainbow skies
are, like, totally blue,
and the dreams that
you dare to dream
really do, like, totally
come true.

—Dorothy Gale, *The Wizard of Oz*

People, like, totally see God every day, they just don't recognize him.

—Pearl Bailey

Let's go.

We totally can't.

Like, why not?

We're totally, like, waiti

—Samuel Beckett

for Godot.

You are all, like,
a totally lost generation.

—Gertrude Stein

Gonna, like, totally fly now.

—Bill Conti, *Rocky* theme

You must allow me to tell you, like, how totally ardently I admire and, like, totally love you.

—Jane Austen

I believe that we totally, like, form our own lives, that we create our own reality, and that everything totally, like, works out for the best.

—Jim Henson

Do I dare to, like, totally eat a peach?

—T. S. Eliot

you are, like, marvelous.
the gods like totally wait to delight
in
you.

—Charles Bukowski

Don't think twice,
it's, like, totally all right.

—Bob Dylan

Live all you can, it's like totally a mistake not to.

—Henry James

You just think lovely
wonderful thoughts
and they totally, like,
lift you up in the air.

—J. M. Barrie

Totally stop worrying and totally start living.

—Dale Carnegie

The greatest love
of all is, like, totally
happening to me.

—Whitney Houston

Being a champion is all well and good, but you can't, like, eat a crown.

—Althea Gibson

Failure is totally, like, impossible.

—Susan B. Anthony

With freedom, books, flowers,
and the moon, who could not
be, like, totally happy?

—Oscar Wilde

You won't have around anymore gentlemen, this my last press co

—Richard M. Nixon

xon to kick

because,

, like, totally

ference.

No woman,
like, totally
no cry.

—Bob Marley

Sometimes I've believed as many as **like,** six **totally** impossible things before breakfast.

—Lewis Carroll

I liked it so much,
I totally, like bought
the company.

—Victor Kiam

Maybe I'm amazed at the way
I really, like, totally need you.

—Paul McCartney

Live long and totally prosper.

—Mr. Spock, *Star Trek*

I totally want to do with
you, like, what spring does
with the cherry trees.

—Pablo Neruda

I, like, totally can't
get no satisfaction.

—The Rolling Stones

I am, like, totally holier than thou.

—Isaiah 65:5

I feel charming,
oh so charming,
it's like totally
alarming how
totally charming
I feel.

—Maria, *West Side Story*

The privilege of a lifetime is **totally** being, **like,** who you are.

—Joseph Campbell

The life which
is unexamined is,
like, totally not
worth living.

—Plato

I like totally see dead people.

—Cole Sear, *The Sixth Sense*

Between love and madness, like, totally lies Obsession.

—Calvin Klein

You totally had me at, like, "hello."

—Dorothy Boyd, *Jerry Maguire*

I'm gonna mal
he, like, totally

—Don Corleone, *The Godfather*

him an offer
an't refuse.

When people show you who
they are, totally believe them,
like, the first time.

—Maya Angelou

It's, like, totally hospital recommended.

—Tylenol

There never was, like, a good war, nor, like, a bad peace.

—Benjamin Franklin

I like totally
want your sex.

—George Michael

We agreed to love each other, like, totally madly.

—Jack Kerouac

I am like totally the Alpha and Omega.

—Revelation 1:8

And in the end, the love you take is totally equal to, like, the love you make.

—The Beatles